World Book's Documenting History
Canadian Independence

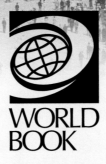

WORLD BOOK

a Scott Fetzer company
Chicago

www.worldbookonline.com

World Book, Inc.
233 N. Michigan Avenue
Chicago, IL 60601
U.S.A.

For information about other World Book publications, visit our website at **http://www.worldbookonline.com**
or call **1-800-WORLDBK (967-5325).**

For information about sales to schools and libraries, call **1-800-975-3250 (United States),** or **1-800-837-5365 (Canada).**

Library of Congress Cataloging-in-Publication Data

Canadian independence.
　　p. cm. -- (World Book's documenting history)
　Includes bibliographical references and index.
　Summary: "A history of the struggle for independence in Canada, based on primary source documents and other historical artifacts. Features include period art works and photographs; excerpts from literary works, letters, speeches, broadcasts, and diaries; summary boxes; a timeline; maps; and a list of additional resources" -- Provided by publisher.
　ISBN 978-0-7166-1502-6　　　8505
　1. Canada--History--1914-1945--Juvenile literature. 2. Canada--Politics and government--1914-1945--Juvenile literature. 3. Canada--History--1914-1945--Sources--Juvenile literature. 4. Canada--Politics and government--1914-1945--Sources--Juvenile literature. I. World Book, Inc.
　F1034.C2457 2011
　971.06--dc22
　　　　　　　　2010016642

World Book's Documenting History
Set ISBN 978-0-7166-1498-2
Printed in Malaysia by TWP Sdn Bhd, JohorBahru
1st printing September 2010

Staff

Executive Committee

Vice President and Chief Financial Officer
　Donald D. Keller
Vice President and Editor in Chief
　Paul A. Kobasa
Vice President, Licensing & Business Development
　Richard Flower
Chief Technology Officer
　Tim Hardy
Managing Director, International
　Benjamin Hinton
Director, Human Resources
　Bev Ecker

Editorial

Associate Director, Supplementary Publications
　Scott Thomas
Senior Editor
　Kristina Vaicikonis
Editor
　Dawn Krajcik

Manager, Contracts & Compliance
(Rights & Permissions)
　Loranne K. Shields
Manager, Research, Supplementary Publications
　Cheryl Graham
Editorial Researcher
　Jon Wills
Administrative Assistant
　Ethel Matthews

Editorial Administration

Director, Systems and Projects
　Tony Tills
Senior Manager, Publishing Operations
　Timothy Falk
Associate Manager, Publishing Operations
　Audrey Casey

Graphics and Design

Manager
　Tom Evans
Coordinator, Design Development and Production
　Brenda B. Tropinski
Senior Designer
　Isaiah W. Sheppard, Jr.
Associate Designer
　Matt Carrington

Production

Director, Manufacturing and Pre-Press
　Carma Fazio
Manufacturing Manager
　Steven K. Hueppchen
Production/Technology Manager
　Anne Fritzinger
Production Specialist
　Curley Hunter
Proofreader
　Emilie Schrage

Marketing

Associate Director, School and Library Marketing
　Jennifer Parello

Produced for World Book by
Arcturus Publishing Limited

Writer: Patience Coster
Editors: Cath Senker, Alex Woolf
Designer: Jane Hawkins

Contents

Canada in World War I

AT THE START OF THE 1900'S, CANADA WAS A *DOMINION* (a self-governing country) within the British Empire. As laid down by the British North America Act of 1867, Canada handled most of its own national issues, and the United Kingdom, also called Britain, handled Canada's foreign affairs. When Britain entered World War I (1914-1918), many Canadians volunteered to fight. However, as the war progressed, Canadians' enthusiasm began to fade. Some Canadians saw the war as a European conflict and resented the huge loss of life among Canadian troops. This resentment grew when troops returned home infected with influenza, which eventually killed about 50,000 Canadians. A sense of national identity and pride also grew out of Canada's war effort.

◀ Canadian combat pilot Billy Bishop (1894-1956) shot down many German planes during World War I. Such heroes fed a sense of Canadian national pride.

▶ John McCrae (1872-1918), a Canadian military surgeon during World War I, wrote *In Flanders Fields* in the spring of 1915. At that time, he was treating soldiers in the trenches near Ypres, Belgium. The poem was first published in the British magazine *Punch* in December 1915. More than 600,000 Canadians served in the war with the Allies (France, Russia, the United Kingdom, and the United States) and about 50,000 died.

In Flanders fields the poppies blow
Between the crosses, row on row,
That mark our place; and in the sky
The larks, still bravely singing, fly
Scarce heard amidst the guns below.
We are the Dead. Short days ago
We lived, felt dawn, saw sunset glow,
Loved, and were loved, and now we lie
In Flanders fields.

from *In Flanders Fields*,
by Lieutenant Colonel
John McCrae

3

But it was European statesmen, European policies and European ambitions that drenched the world in blood.... Fifty thousand Canadian soldiers under the soil of France and Flanders is what Canada has paid for European statesmanship.

Newton W. Rowell, 1920

◀ Newton Wesley Rowell (1867-1941), a Canadian lawyer and statesman, addressed the first Assembly of the League of Nations in Geneva, Switzerland, in December 1920. The League of Nations was an organization of nations created to maintain peace after World War I. During his speech, Rowell stressed that the League was a world, and not only a European, organization.

▼ The *Taking of Vimy Ridge, Easter Monday 1917,* a painting by British artist Richard Jack (1866-1952). The Battle of Vimy Ridge was a great victory for Canada in World War I. The careful planning and heroism of the Canadian Corps led to the defeat of the German Sixth Army. About 3,600 Canadians died in the battle, and more than 7,000 others were wounded.

4

NOW YOU KNOW

- At the start of the 1900's, Britain controlled Canadian foreign affairs.
- As a dominion of the British Empire, Canada entered World War I on the side of the Allies.
- The huge number of Canadian deaths resulting from the war and from influenza made many Canadians resent British control over Canada.

Postwar Identity

THE EXPERIENCE OF WORLD WAR I MADE CANADA'S LEADERS REALIZE the disadvantage of having its foreign policy determined by Britain. In 1919, at the signing of the Treaty of Versailles (the postwar peace settlement), Canada insisted on representing itself. Prime Minister Sir Robert Borden, as well as the leaders of other dominion countries, signed the peace treaty independently. In 1920, Canada and the other dominions joined the League of Nations as *charter* (original) members. Fearing future involvement in European wars, the Canadian government tried in the early 1920's to remove guarantees that Canada would support its allies militarily if their security were threatened. However, its attempts to remove these guarantees failed.

▲ The Canadian delegates, seated before their secretaries, to the first Assembly of the League of Nations in 1920 in Geneva, Switzerland: *left to right,* Loring C. Christie, Charles Joseph Doherty, Georges E. Foster, and Newton Wesley Rowell. The League of Nations was an international association of countries created to keep peace after World War I. The League Assembly included delegates from all member nations. It met every year to discuss issues of world peace, to pass *resolutions* (formal expressions of opinion), and to create committees to investigate international problems.

2

It can hardly be expected that we shall put 400,000 or 500,000 men in the field and willingly accept the position of having no more voice and receiving no more consideration than if we were toy automata [robots].

Robert Borden, 1916

◀ In a letter to George Perley (1857-1938), Canadian Acting High Commissioner in London, Canadian Prime Minister Robert Borden (1854-1937) warns that Britain should not take Canada's sacrifice for granted. Borden led Canada during World War I. In 1917, his government enacted the *conscription* (forced military service) of Canadian soldiers.

▶ The "Canada" article in *The World Book Encyclopedia Annual for 1922* described a new sense of Canadian national identity following World War I. Canada emerged from the war determined to establish its independence. In 1922, Canada's government refused to support Britain in a possible war with Turkey. In 1923, Canada for the first time signed a treaty alone with another country—the United States. The treaty regulated fishing in the Pacific Ocean.

3

Outstanding in the history of Canada is the growing consciousness of nationality. The reason for this is obvious to a Canadian, if not to an outsider. The great crisis of the war showed what the Canadians were and what they could do—showed not only the world but, much more important, themselves.

from *The World Book Encyclopedia Annual for 1922*

NOW YOU KNOW

- Canada emerged from World War I with a sense of national pride and the determination to establish its independence.
- In 1919, Canada signed the Treaty of Versailles independently of Britain.
- In 1920, Canada joined the League of Nations.

The One Big Union

WHEN THE WAR ENDED IN 1918, ALMOST 300,000 CANADIANS LOST THEIR JOBS in war-related industries. It was hard for men returning from military service to find work. In March 1919, representatives from local labor unions across western Canada met in Calgary, Alberta, and expressed support for the advancement of workers' rights. They decided to form a labor organization called the One Big Union (OBU). Thousands of workers, including many in the mining, railway, and logging industries, joined the OBU. The Canadian government and business community were alarmed. After Communists took control of Russia in the Russian Revolution of 1917, Canada's government feared the growth of social unrest at home.

▲ Men work in a coal mine in Alberta in the 1920's. During the 1920's, mining companies, backed by the government, crushed workers' strikes protesting wage cuts and poor working conditions in Alberta, British Columbia, and Nova Scotia.

▶ A report by the Methodist Church in 1918 expressed a belief in the need for economic reform. Some Protestant groups believed that the main causes of unrest after the war were inequalities of wealth and opportunity and the merciless pursuit of profits by big businesses.

The war has made more clearly *manifest* [apparent] the moral perils *inherent* [deeply rooted] in the system of production for profits. . . . Under the shock and strain of this tremendous struggle, accepted commercial and industrial methods based on *individualism* [the belief in individual freedom] and competition have gone down like mud walls in a flood.

from the 1918 report of the Methodist Church

3

Modern industrial society is divided into two classes, those who possess and do not produce, and those who produce and do not possess. . . . Between these two classes a continual struggle takes place. . . . there exists a struggle on the one hand of the buyer to buy as cheaply as possible, and on the other, of the seller to sell for as much as possible, so with the buyers and sellers of labor power. In the struggle over the purchase and sale of labor power the buyers are always masters—the sellers always workers.

from the One Big Union constitution, 1919

◀ The constitution of the OBU expressed a belief in an ongoing conflict between workers and employers. Although many people in government viewed such beliefs as dangerous, others agreed that industry should be reformed. The reform-minded felt that it was important to hold back competitiveness and increase cooperation to bring peace and stability to the workplace.

▶ The "giant" of the OBU strikes out for workers' rights in a prolabor cartoon. The I.W.W. on the giant's apron refers to the Industrial Workers of the World, a radical labor organization that wanted to abolish capitalism. The I.W.W. organized the OBU. At its peak in 1920, the OBU had about 50,000 members. However, disagreements within the OBU and a campaign against it by government and employers limited the union's power. By 1923, it had been reduced to about 5,000 members.

4

NOW YOU KNOW

- The end of World War I left many Canadians without jobs.
- In 1919, Canadian workers created a leftist labor organization called the One Big Union.
- The government feared that union activity might bring about a revolution.

The Winnipeg Strike

IN POSTWAR CANADA, *INFLATION* (RISING PRICES) LED TO A FALL IN LIVING STANDARDS. Many Canadian businesses had made huge profits producing goods for World War I. Yet wages and working conditions for ordinary people were poor. On May 15, 1919, thousands of workers in Winnipeg, Manitoba, walked out of their jobs, and the city ground to a halt. As other strikes took place across the country, the government decided to take action. On June 21, later called "Bloody Saturday," soldiers and mounted police in Winnipeg charged a crowd of strikers, killing one and wounding dozens of others. The strike was called off on June 25.

◀ Mounted police charge through the center of Winnipeg in June 1919, during the Winnipeg General Strike.

▶ An article published in the May 16, 1919, edition of *The (Montreal) Gazette* describes the magnitude of the Winnigpeg General Strike. The federal government and citizens groups worked to keep the province's services running, and the strike failed. However, it did much to bring attention to workers' rights in the emerging economy.

Winnipeg is now in the *throes* [pangs] of the greatest labor struggle of all her history. Estimates vary as to the total number of workers out on strike, these running from 15,000 to 27,000.

The mayor and city council are grappling with the problem of maintaining the essential services of public utilities, police and fire protection as the tie-up grows. Every walk of industrial and commercial life in Winnipeg is represented among the strikers.

The (Montreal) Gazette,
May 16, 1919

3

The ONE BIG UNION is Bolshevism Pure and Simple

NOTE THE STRIKING PARALLEL

Bolshevism

... the constitution of "The Federation of Unions of Russia ... the U.S. and Canada," the simon pure Bolshevik organization plant ... by paid agents of Lenine and Trotzky.

One Big Union

Extract from the official stenographic record of the proceedings at the Western Canada Labor Conference at Calgary last March, where the One Big Union movement was launched by labor delegates from all western cities, including 29 from Winnipeg.

4

Any association . . . whose professed purpose . . . is to bring about any governmental, industrial or economic change within Canada by use of force, violence or physical injury to person or property, or by threats of such injury, or which teaches, *advocates* [supports], advises or defends the use of force, violence, terrorism, or physical injury to person or property . . . in order to accomplish such change, or for any other purpose, or which shall by any means persecute or pursue such purpose . . . or shall so teach, advocate, advise or defend, shall be an unlawful association.

Section 98 of the Criminal Code, 1919

▲ A newspaper headline compares the OBU with Bolshevism, the Russian Communist movement. Opponents of the OBU claimed it was a hotbed of revolutionaries. The refusal of Canadian employers to recognize unions as lawful denied most workers the chance to voice their concerns. The OBU was created while the Winnipeg General Strike was taking place.

◄ Canada's Criminal Code was revised in 1919 after the Winnipeg General Strike. Changes to the code expanded its definition of sedition, the act of stirring up discontent against established government authority.

NOW YOU KNOW

- Many Canadians worked for low wages in poor conditions after World War I.
- In 1919, the Winnipeg General Strike brought the city to a standstill and ended in violence.
- After the strike, Canada's federal government passed a law that banned organizations that wanted to overthrow capitalism.

The Great Head Count

THE CANADIAN GOVERNMENT BEGAN CONDUCTING ITS SIXTH NATIONAL CENSUS on June 1, 1921. The 1921 census reported a total population of nearly nine million. The most significant trend in the 10 years since the previous census was the migration of people to cities. Since 1881, every Canadian census had reported an increased migration from the countryside to cities. Canada's rural population also had grown because of the expansion of agriculture in the Prairie Provinces—Manitoba, Saskatchewan, and Alberta. By 1921, the population was about equally divided between urban and rural areas.

◀ The Feb. 24, 1922, *Toronto Daily Star* printed the results of Canada's 1921 census by province and compared them with the results of the 1911 census.

▼ Robert Hamilton Coats (1874-1960) describes the 1921 census. Coats became Canada's first dominion statistician and controller of the census in 1915. In 1918, he helped establish the Dominion Bureau of Statistics. Coats oversaw the large staff that processed information from the 1921 census. The census showed that British Canadians made up more than half of the population and that French Canadians made up more than one-fourth of it.

This census is the largest peacetime operation ever organized by the Canadian government . . . nothing less than a great periodical stock-taking of the people and their affairs.

Robert Hamilton Coats,
dominion statistician

3

Measured by the history of most nations, Canada in organized form is but an infant, for slightly more than half way between the census of 1911 and 1921 it passed its fiftieth year since Confederation—since the Dominion was organized. Its present political status dates from 1867. On July 1, 1867, there were but 3,000,000 people in this vast territory, and the census of 1921 shows that the increase has been about threefold. Hope had been expressed that the census of 1921 would show more than 10,000,000 people, but the war disappointed such ambitions.

from the *World Book Encyclopedia Annual for 1922*

▲ The "Canada" article in *The World Book Encyclopedia Annual for 1922* blamed lower-than-hoped-for population growth on World War I.

4

◀ Midday traffic in Toronto, 1924. In the late 1800's and early 1900's, the number of people moving to cities increased. For the first time, Canada had two cities, Toronto and Montreal, each with a population of more than 500,000.

NOW YOU KNOW

- The 1921 Canadian census reported a population of nearly 9 million people.
- The census showed that city populations were growing quickly.
- Canadians of British descent formed a majority of the population. French Canadians made up the second largest group.

Cultural Conflict

THROUGHOUT ITS EARLY HISTORY, CANADA WAS TROUBLED BY A lack of unity among its people. Cultural and religious differences led to disagreements about government policies. English-speaking Protestants held most of the power in Canada, even in Quebec, where French-speaking Roman Catholics made up the majority. Many French Canadians supported a movement to make Quebec a separate nation. They objected to reforms, introduced and passed by English-speaking Canadians, that expressed *bias* (prejudice) against their traditional way of life. In 1912, for example, Ontario's government passed "Regulation 17," which limited the use of French in public schools.

▶ Members of Ottawa's English-speaking upper classes attend a garden party hosted by Lord Bessborough, governor general of Canada from 1931 to 1935. The governor general represents the British monarch. English-speaking Canadians had greater economic and political power than French Canadians did in the early 1900's.

▼ Liberal politician Joseph-Napoléon Francoeur (1880-1965) introduced a *resolution* (formal opinion) in Quebec's Legislative Assembly in 1918 that expressed a willingness to separate Quebec from the Dominion of Canada. At that time, the Legislative Assembly was the lower house of Quebec's legislature.

That this House is of [the] opinion that the Province of Quebec would be *disposed* [inclined] to accept the breaking of the Confederation pact of 1867 if, in the other Provinces, it is believed that she is an obstacle to the Union, progress and development of Canada.

Legislative Assembly of Quebec, 1918

3 Our special task, as French Canadians, is to insert into America the spirit of Christian France. It is to defend against all comers, perhaps even against France herself, our religious and national heritage. This heritage does not belong to us alone. It belongs to all Catholic America. It is the inspiring and shining hearth of America. It belongs to the whole Church, and it is the basic foundation of the Church in this part of the world. It belongs to all French civilization of which it is the *refuge* [shelter] and fortress and anchor amid the immense sea of *saxonizing* [making British] Americanism.

Henri Bourassa, *Le Devoir* newspaper, 1918

◀ Roman Catholicism was a central element of French Canadian culture. *Le Devoir* was an influential Montreal newspaper founded by Henri Bourassa (1868-1952) in 1910. Bourassa, a French Canadian journalist and political leader, fought for the equality of the English and French languages and cultures in Canada. He also supported greater Canadian independence from the United Kingdom. Bourassa served in the Canadian House of Commons and in the Quebec legislature during the late 1800's and early 1900's.

4

▶ A French-Canadian man pulls a cart loaded with tobacco leaves in 1920. In the early 1900's, most people of French ancestry in Canada were from farming back-grounds and had little political power. They struggled to preserve their culture in a society dominated by the British Canadian upper classes.

NOW YOU KNOW

- Cultural differences caused problems for Canada from its early history.
- British Canadians held most of the economic and political power in Canada during the late 1800's and early 1900's.
- Many French Canadians wanted to make the province of Quebec a separate country.

Liberals and Progressives

I N THE FEDERAL GENERAL ELECTION OF DEC. 6, 1921, the Liberal Party won the most seats in the House of Commons but fell just short of a majority. The Progressive Party, a new political party associated with farmers in western Canada, won the second most seats in the House. The Conservative Party, one of Canada's two main traditional parties, won the third most seats. For the first time in Canadian history, no single party had a majority. The Liberals had to rely upon the support of the Progressives to govern. The Progressive Party did not survive past the 1930's, but it was important because it ended the domination of Canadian politics by two main parties.

◀ William Lyon Mackenzie King (1874-1950) led the Liberal Party of Canada for 29 years, from 1919 to 1948. He served as prime minister of Canada three times—from 1921 to 1926, 1926 to 1930, and 1935 to 1948; and he held the office for more years than anybody else. As prime minister, King worked to enhance Canadian self-government in foreign relations and to unite English-speaking and French-speaking Canadians.

2

▶ Thomas Alexander Crerar (1876-1975), a former Liberal, led the Progressive Party from 1920 to 1922. The Progressives' focus was on protecting Canadian farmers' interests. One of their main goals during the 1921 election was free trade with the United States. An existing *tariff* (tax) forced farmers to sell their products at lower prices and import farm tools at higher prices. However, the tariff protected central Canadian industry.

Our appeal is not class, not sectional, not religious. . . . [instead we seek the support of all] who desire to see purity in the government restored, who desire to see public morality supplant [replace] public corruption, who desire to sweep away abuse of the function of government for the advancement of the interest of the privileged few.

Thomas Crerar, 1920

3

Never in Canada have the devotees of law and order received a ruder shock. . . . The lesson is obvious yet it should be stated. Any government which attempts to throttle free men in Canada or elsewhere will fall of its own weight and be fortunate if it does not bring crashing in ruin the structure which with clumsy hands it seeks to *buttress* [shore up].

from *Canadian Forum*, October 1920

◀ The political journal *Canadian Forum* characterizes the outcome of the 1920 Manitoba general election: "Any government which attempts to *throttle* (beat down) free men . . . will fall. . . ." As in federal politics, Manitoba politics exhibited a movement away from the two-party system. Growing support for farmers', labor, and socialist candidates took votes away from the Liberals and Conservatives, and the Liberals failed to win a majority of seats in Manitoba's legislature in 1920. Four men elected to the Assembly that year were in prison because of their involvement with the Winnipeg General Strike (see pages 10-11).

NOW YOU KNOW

- In 1921, the Liberal Party won Canada's general election without winning a majority of seats in the House of Commons.
- For the first time, no single party controlled the Canadian House of Commons.
- The Progressive Party ended two-party federal politics in Canada.

The Mid-1920's Boom

CANADA'S ECONOMY EXPERIENCED A BRIEF RECESSION FROM 1920 TO 1922. Following this recession, the economy began to expand. The development of forest and mineral resources was an important reason for this expansion. In the financial sector, the price of stocks on the stock market rose steadily from 1921 to 1929. In addition, the price of everyday goods fell, and so people had more buying power, even though wages increased little or remained the same. Smuggling alcohol from Canada to the United States, which still had laws banning liquor, became a profitable business for some people. However, the boom of the mid-1920's benefited Canadians unevenly. Certain parts of the country experienced less economic growth than others. In particular, the Prairie and Maritime provinces fared worse than did the central provinces of Ontario and Quebec.

▲ A family skis near Toronto, Ontario. A decrease in the cost of living in the 1920's enabled ordinary Canadians to stretch their money further. In the summer, many Canadians "took to the woods," visiting holiday resorts or building cottages next to lakes along the edge of the Canadian Shield region.

▶ Tom Moore, president of the Trades and Labour Congress of Canada, comments on the financial difficulties faced by poorer Canadians in the mid-1920's. Not all Canadians benefited equally from the economic expansion that took place during this period.

Years ago, a man, even though his pay was smaller, could look forward to something. It was possible to save, and it didn't need a great deal to set up a home....
Now everything seems against the young fellow with domestic ideas.
Tom Moore, 1925

3

Searching out makers of *moonshine* [liquor made unlawfully or smuggled] in Alberta costs the provincial liquor control board more than $15,000 a year. This work might well be done by the federal police, particularly in view of the fact that the Dominion takes nearly two and one-half millions a year in revenue as a result of the manufacture and sale of liquor in Alberta. . . . the province proposes to deal with the situation arising from the operations of a private wholesale liquor house in Fernie. . . . It is expected that the Alberta representatives will attempt to establish before the board that liquor is crossing the line from Fernie to Alberta and is making its way from Fernie to the United States through this province.

The Calgary Daily Herald, Jan. 27, 1927

◄ The *Calgary Daily Herald* newspaper describes the high cost of fighting liquor smuggling in the late 1920's. Both Canada and the United States had Prohibition laws that banned liquor during the early 1900's. After World War I, Canadian opposition to Prohibition grew, partly because Canadians wanted to make money by smuggling alcohol into the United States.

4

► Canadian authorities raid an illegal liquor factory in Elk Lake, Ontario, in 1921. Most Canadian provinces had Prohibition laws by 1918. Individual provinces began to abolish Prohibition in 1921. The United States did not abolish Prohibition until 1933.

NOW YOU KNOW

- Overall, Canada's economy expanded in the 1920's.
- The economic growth that began in the mid-1920's did not affect all regions of Canada equally.
- Smuggling liquor from Canada to the United States, where Prohibition lasted longer, became a profitable business for some people.

Rural Complaints

THE SETTLEMENT OF WESTERN CANADA INCREASED WITH the construction of great railroads that crossed the continent in the 1800's. Villages and small towns sprang up across the prairies. Life in the rural Prairie Provinces—Alberta, Manitoba, and Saskatchewan—was harsh, and local people had to cooperate with one another to survive. Farmers' groups felt that the government did not help them. They complained about the great expense of transporting goods, the high prices of farm tools, and the low prices that merchants paid for their grain. The Progressive Party grew out of these farmers' groups, which included United Farmers parties in a number of provinces.

1

To protect the farmer. To obtain complete control of the main Canadian produce. To market our crops under our own system. To *affiliate* [join] with all the farmer organizations of the world, with one central *executive* [manager] in each country, which will fix prices according to a fair average of estimates sent in by the locals, will through the same source also know amount of marketable produce in the country; will have to keep informed as to the demands and needs of importing countries, and will also help to prevent the re-occurrence of *famine* [food shortage] . . .

from the Constitution and Laws
of the Farmers' Union of Canada

◀ The constitution of the Farmers' Union of Canada was based on the constitution of the One Big Union (see pages 8-9). The first convention of the Farmers' Union took place in Saskatoon, Saskatchewan, on July 25, 1922. The union's goals included protecting agricultural interests and uniting farmers' groups around the world.

2

▶ Farmers harvest wheat with a combine in Vulcan, Alberta. The community of Vulcan developed along the route of the Canadian Pacific Railway in the early 1900's. Area wheat farmers stored their crops in grain elevators in Vulcan, where trains stopped to collect it. Vulcan once boasted nine giant grain elevators, known as the "nine in a line." Today only one elevator remains.

▼ *The Progressive*, the newspaper of the Progressive Party, describes a "class struggle" in which farmers and buyers of produce compete to control the sale of agricultural products. The Progressive Party, which developed out of farmers' organizations in western Canada, had strong support in the Prairie Provinces and Ontario.

4

The "class struggle," as affecting the farmers, means, in the first place, that in the struggle over the sale of farm produce, the buyers are always the masters. . . . These people, through organization, have secured control over the store-houses and *elevators* [buildings for storing grain] . . . They have selling agencies, bureaus of information, through which they keep in touch with the world-buyers; with them they bargain and so market their wealth.

from *The Progressive*,
July 3, 1924

3

▲ Henry Wise Wood (1860-1941) led the United Farmers of Alberta from 1916 to 1931. He became a leader of Alberta's wheat pool movement of 1923-1924. Wheat pools were businesses owned and operated by groups of farmers to handle the sale of their grain. The pools developed after the federal government in 1920 disbanded the Canadian Wheat Board, an agency that had regulated the grain trade. Through the wheat pool movement, Wood promoted his vision of strong farmers' organizations that could stand up to bankers, industrialists, and professionals.

NOW YOU KNOW

- Life was difficult for farmers in the Prairie Provinces.
- Western farmers felt that the government did little to help them.
- Farmers organized the United Farmers movement and the Farmers' Union of Canada to protect their interests and gain more control over agriculture.

Agriculture and Resources

AGRICULTURE EXPANDED IN CANADA DURING THE 1920's. However, the price of wheat, a leading export, fell from 1921 to 1929. Many farmers in the Prairie Provinces of Alberta, Manitoba, and Saskatchewan had borrowed money to expand their production during World War I. After the war, they could not afford to pay back their loans or maintain all their lands. A lack of rainfall during the 1920's also caused problems for prairie farmers. As the 1920's progressed, wood pulp, used to make paper, surpassed wheat as Canada's top export. Large pulp and paper mills sprang up in Ontario and British Columbia to supply the United States with newsprint. Canadian mines in the Canadian Shield region also supplied American industries with metals such as as copper, gold, iron, nickel, and zinc.

▲ Deserted farm buildings in Saskatchewan. During World War I, the demand for Canadian wheat was great. Many farmers borrowed money and expanded their farms into regions that were too dry. After the war, these farmers could not afford to pay back their loans or maintain their expanded farms. Many had to abandon their fields.

▶ The World Book Encyclopedia Annual describes Canada's record 1928 wheat crop. Larger yields helped to make up for lower grain prices during the 1920's. Canada's share of the grain market increased in the late 1920's, because European and Soviet farmers were not producing as much as they had before World War I and the Russian Revolution of 1917.

Agricultural production also showed a marked increase over the output of 1927. The Prairie Provinces realized an enormous grain crop, despite severe weather *handicaps* [disadvantages]. The wheat yield was the largest recorded in Canada.

from *The World Book Encyclopedia Annual for 1928.*

3

4

> . . . the interest of the Crown in all Crown lands, mines, minerals (precious and base) and *royalties* [money paid to the landowner] derived therefrom within the Province, and all sums due or payable for such lands, mines, minerals or royalties, shall . . . belong to the Province, subject to any trusts existing in respect thereof, and to any interest other than that of the Crown in the same, and the said lands, mines, minerals and royalties shall be administered by the Province. . . .
>
> Alberta Natural Resources Act, 1930

▲ Fraser Mills, in British Columbia, was the largest sawmill in the British Empire during the early 1900's. Immigrants from Britain, eastern Canada, China, India, Japan, Scandinavia, and the United States provided the mill with cheap labor.

◀ The Alberta Natural Resources Act, passed by the Canadian Parliament in 1930, transferred ownership of natural resources from the federal government to the province. Similar acts passed at the same time transferred natural resources to British Columbia, Manitoba, and Saskatchewan. Before confederation, the United Kingdom had owned these resources. These transfers enriched primarily rural provinces.

NOW YOU KNOW

- Overall, Canadian agriculture expanded during the 1920's, but wheat prices fell.
- Wood pulp overtook wheat as Canada's chief export during the 1920's.
- In 1930, the United Kingdom gave several provinces greater rights over local natural resources.

The Maritime Provinces

THE ECONOMY OF THE MARITIME PROVINCES—New Brunswick, Nova Scotia, and Prince Edward Island—suffered from a decline in the fishing, iron and steel, manufacturing, and mining industries during the postwar recession. The mid-1920's boom that helped central Canada recover from the recession did not bring prosperity to the Maritime Provinces. During the 1920's, many Maritimers felt anger toward the federal government because its economic policies benefited the central provinces and harmed Maritime interests. They felt that they were making sacrifices to enrich "Upper Canadians"—a name used to describe the wealthy residents of the former British colony called Upper Canada (now Ontario). Some people thought that the Maritime Provinces should separate from the dominion and control their own affairs.

◀ Men working at the Dominion Iron and Steel Company in Sydney, Nova Scotia. A drop in iron and steel prices in the early 1920's hurt the Maritime Provinces' iron and steel industries.

▶ In his novel *This Thing Called Love* (1929), author Louis Arthur Cunningham (1900-1954) wrote about economic conditions in the Maritime Provinces in the 1920's. During the first three decades of the 1900's, such poor conditions motivated hundreds of thousands of people to emigrate from the Maritime Provinces. This population decrease had the effect of decreasing the Maritime Provinces' representation in Parliament, where economic policy was made.

Year after year the drab banner of poverty flaps in the breeze and the local *Tageblatt* [a newspaper] announces that prosperity—strange, *elusive* [hard to get] thing—is coming. How can it come? We have few industries, few factories, a pitiful few that struggle for *ignoble* [disgraceful] existence, that underpay their hands, that are treadmills. Thousands of our native-born have gone; not led by the *lure* [attraction] of big money, but merely by the hope of making a fair and honest living.

Louis Arthur Cunningham, 1929

3 ◀ Miners in the Malagash Salt Mine in Malagash, Nova Scotia. From 1918, the mine was a major source of employment in that area. A local poet whose name is unknown highlighted the mine's importance in the following lines:

"When you're out of a job & haven't a dime,

It's two days a week at the Malagash Mine."

▶ An open letter written in 1924 by New Brunswick businessman Lewis Connors blamed banks for the economic failure of many manufacturing companies during the 1920's. Financial institutions had taken over Connors' own sardine-canning company, Connors Brothers, Limited. Connors' letter urges the Canadian government to stimulate business by helping manufacturers secure loans.

4 *When times were good a few years ago banks were very liberal in lending money. . . . As soon as times changed—and I might say this was the cause of the change—the banks closed up very tight and in a short time a lot of firms were bankrupt [bust], causing hard times and driving people out of the country. This was largely the cause of so many members dropping out of the [Canadian Manufacturers' Association], their business having been closed up and sold but by the banks, mortgages or parties to whom they owed money. . . . I think the Government should take some means with the banking whereby money should be loaned to good honest people, in Canada so that they may get business going. Manufacturing business means prosperity.*

Lewis Connors, 1924

NOW YOU KNOW

- The economic boom of the mid-1920's did not bring prosperity to the Maritime Provinces.
- In the 1920's, many Maritimers resented the economic policies of the federal government.
- Some people in the Maritimes called for regional self-government.

Industry and Energy

WOOD PULP AND PAPER PRODUCTION GREW RAPIDLY DURING THE 1920's in British Columbia, Ontario, and Quebec. By 1929, Canada produced 65 percent of the world's exports of newsprint. Canadian mining also expanded quickly in British Columbia, Manitoba, Ontario, and Quebec. From 1918 to 1923, Canada was the second largest producer of automobiles in the world, after the United States. Canada's mountains and rivers provided a good opportunity for producing hydroelectric power, and Canadian industry became more and more dependent upon hydroelectric power and less dependent on coal. Hydroelectric power allowed pulp and paper mills to operate in remote northern locations.

1

Since the first water turbine was installed near Hamilton, Ont., about thirty years ago, the production and consumption of hydroelectric power in the Dominion has practically doubled every seven years. The total amount developed up to the present time is over 5,000,000 horse power [3.7 million kilowatts].

from *The World Book Encyclopedia Annual for 1929*

▲ An article in the *World Book Encyclopedia Annual* describes the growing significance of hydroelectric power in Canada in the early 1900's. Access to cheap hydroelectric power was very important to Canada's pulp and paper industries. The increased use of hydroelectric power in central Canada hurt the coal industry in Atlantic Canada.

▶ A hydroelectric power plant in Beauharnois, Quebec, in the early 1930's. Hydroelectric plants use moving water to spin large *turbines* (engines) connected to *generators*. Generators change mechanical energy into electric energy.

2

3

▶ A Canadian periodical describes the essential role of the automobile industry in Canadian life in the 1930's. Thousands of Canadians had jobs assembling and servicing automobiles and manufacturing tires and other spare parts.

. . . the motor vehicle industry is so bound up in the social, commercial and industrial life of the country that there is scarcely an industry that does not benefit directly or indirectly.

Canadian Geographical Journal,
April 1937

▼ The Gove Motor Car Company in Tilbury, Ontario, was an American branch plant (see pages 28-29) where the Falcon Light Six automobile was manufactured. During the 1920's, a Canadian tax on imported cars made it more cost effective for American car companies to manufacture cars in Canada than to export them there. Such companies as Chrysler, Ford, and General Motors had Canadian factories.

4

NOW YOU KNOW

- Pulp and paper production and mining grew rapidly in Canada in the 1920's.
- Canada was the world's second largest automobile producer from 1918 to 1923.
- Hydroelectric power became increasingly important in Canada in the early 1900's.

American Branch Plants

THE ESTABLISHMENT OF AMERICAN BRANCH PLANTS IN CANADA strengthened ties between Canada and the United States in the 1920's. Branch plants were companies set up in Canada and run by parent companies in the United States. By producing goods in Canada, American firms avoided paying transportation costs and *tariffs* (import taxes). The first important branch plants in Canada made newsprint. Mining companies, grocery-store chains, and other kinds of businesses also established branches in Canada. Some Canadians believed that American investment would help develop and strengthen Canada's economy. Others feared an economic takeover by the United States.

▲ The Hudson Bay Mining and Smelting Company, in Flin Flon, Manitoba, was controlled by the H. P. Whitney Company of New York City. In the 1920's, Canada experienced a mining boom. From 1921 to 1929, silver production doubled and gold production tripled. Production of such *base* (nonprecious) metals as lead, nickel, and zinc quadrupled. By 1930, companies controlled by Americans owned nearly 40 percent of Canada's mineral production.

2

▶ Addressing thousands of Canadians in Vancouver, British Columbia, during a presidential visit, U.S. President Warren G. Harding (1865-1923) commented on how the economies of Canada and the United States were interconnected. By 1930, direct investment in Canada by the United States was more than five times the amount of investment by the United Kingdom.

We think the same thoughts, live the same lives, and cherish the same aspirations [goals]. . . . A further evidence of our increasing inter-dependence appears in the shifting of capital [business funds]. Since the Armistice [end of war in 1918] . . . approximately $2,500,000,000 has found its way from the United States into Canada for investment. That is a huge sum of money and I have no doubt it is employed safely for us and helpfully for you.
U.S. President
Warren G. Harding, 1923

3

◀ The headquarters of the Ford Motor Company of Canada, Limited, in London, Ontario, in the 1920's. American companies operated branch plants so they could avoid paying tariffs on exports to Canada. Americans often held the top management jobs in the branch plants, and company profits usually flowed back to the United States.

NOW YOU KNOW

- American companies set up branch plants in Canada to avoid paying tariffs and transportation costs on their products.
- By 1930, American investment in Canadian industry was much higher than British investment.
- Canadians had mixed feelings about American investment in Canada.

Labor and the Social Gospel

IN 1921, TWO MEMBERS OF PROVINCIAL LABOR PARTIES—James Shaver Woodsworth (1874-1942) of Winnipeg and William Irvine (1885-1962) of Calgary—won seats in the Canadian Parliament. Both were Protestant ministers and part of the Social Gospel movement, which tried to apply Christian teachings to society's problems. Woodsworth and Irvine wanted churches and the government to become more active on such social issues as alcohol abuse, the hardships of immigrants, labor conditions, poverty, and prostitution. Canada's health care system, social and welfare services, unemployment assistance, and workers' compensation have their roots in the Social Gospel movement.

▶ Methodist minister and labor politician J. S. Woodsworth speaks at a meeting in 1935. Described as the "conscience of Canada," Woodsworth worked to help immigrants in Canadian cities and supported the right of trade unions to negotiate pay levels with employers. He was arrested for his involvement in the Winnipeg General Strike of 1919.

2

Our ultimate *objective* [goal] must be a complete turnover in the present economic and social system. . . .

J. S. Woodsworth, *Western Labor News,* July 18, 1919

The fight is not between hand workers and brain workers. It is not between industrial workers and agricultural workers. The fight is essentially between the producers and the *parasites* [those who live on others].

J. S. Woodsworth, *Western Labor News,* July 25, 1919

◀ In 1919, the *Western Labor News* printed a series of articles by J. S. Woodsworth that called the owners of capital and industry "parasites." Woodsworth's slogan in the 1921 federal election campaign was "Human needs before property rights." As a Member of Parliament, he worked to focus awareness on the needs of the elderly, farmers, immigrants, and the jobless.

3

What we want is a national union covering each industry in Canada, which will be fully organized and . . . strong enough to take a share in the control as well as the profits of industry.

Aaron R. Mosher, 1929

◀ The president of the All-Canadian Congress of Labour, Aaron Roland Mosher (1881-1959), describes his vision for organized labor. In the early 1920's, labor union membership fell dramatically. This decline occurred partly because American branch plant owners worked hard to prevent unions from organizing employees in their plants. The creation of the All-Canadian Congress of Labour in 1926 joined unions into a kind of league to try to improve the fortunes of the labor movement and the lives of its members.

▶ Government representatives present the first old-age pension check to a man from British Columbia in 1927. J. S. Woodsworth and fellow labor Member of Parliament Abraham Albert Heaps (1885-1954) pushed the government to establish Canada's first old-age pension plan. The plan became the basis of Canada's social security system.

4

NOW YOU KNOW

- In 1921, Canadians elected labor candidates J. S. Woodsworth and William Irvine to Parliament.
- Labor politicians and the Social Gospel movement promoted the rights of farmers, immigrants, and workers.
- The Canadian welfare system has its roots in the Social Gospel movement.

Loosening Ties

AFTER THE SIGNING OF THE TREATY OF VERSAILLES IN 1919, Canada continued to withdraw gradually from involvement with the United Kingdom. In September 1922, British Prime Minister Lloyd George called upon Canada and other dominion countries to support the United Kindom in a potential war against Turkey. He wanted Canadian soldiers to help the British hold a position at the Turkish port of Chanak. This request angered Prime Minister Mackenzie King, who dodged it by saying that the Canadian Parliament was on holiday. At the 1923 Imperial Conference in London, King opposed having a common foreign policy for all the British Empire.

1

. . . as regards European wars. . . . I have thought out my plans. . . . No [army] contingent will go without parliament being summoned [called] in the first instance. . . . I do not believe prlt. [parliament] would sanction the sending of a contingent. . . . The French Canadians will be opposed, I am not so sure of B. C. [British Columbia]—I feel confident the Progressives will be opposed almost to a man. It is the time now to bring them into the Government. . . . I am sure the people of Canada are against participation in this European war.

from Prime Minister Mackenzie King's diary, September 17, 1922

◀ An entry in Prime Minister Mackenzie King's diary expresses King's unwillingness to send Canadian troops to Turkey. By refusing to help the British at Chanak, King showed that Canada wanted a say in its own foreign policy. In public, King said that he could not offer military support to Britain without first consulting Canada's Parliament.

2

When Britain's message came, then Canada should have said: "Ready, aye Ready; we stand by you."
Arthur Meighen, 1922

▶ Speaking in Toronto on Sept. 22, 1922, Conservative Party leader and former Prime Minister Arthur Meighen (1874-1960) argued that Mackenzie King should have offered military support to Britain. He echoed the feelings of many British Canadians. When the Chanak crisis was over, Meighen was left with a reputation for blindly following British orders.

◀ Canadian fishermen cleaning fish, 1916. In 1923, Canada signed the Halibut Treaty with the United States to regulate fishing in the Atlantic and Pacific oceans and the Great Lakes. The treaty was the first that Canada signed alone with another country. Britain had co-signed previous treaties.

▲ Senior politicians from the United Kingdom and dominion countries gathered in London in 1923 for an Imperial Conference. The dominion and British representatives agreed that the dominions had the right to make treaties without consulting the British government. This *concession* (yielding) by Britain was a direct outcome of the Canadian-American fisheries treaty.

NOW YOU KNOW

- In 1922, Canada refused to support Britain in a potential war with Turkey.
- Canada independently signed the Halibut Treaty with the United States in 1923.
- Representatives at the 1923 Imperial Conference agreed that the dominions could make treaties without consulting Britain.

The 1925 Election

I N THE GENERAL ELECTION OF OCT. 29, 1925, the Conservatives won 116 out of 245 seats in the House of Commons. The Liberals won only 99 seats. However, as was his constitutional right, Prime Minister Mackenzie King opted not to hand over power to the Conservatives, who had not won a majority of House seats. Instead, King decided to remain in office with the support of the Progressives, who had secured 24 seats in the House. About six months after the election, corruption was revealed in the customs ministry. Customs officials had accepted bribes to overlook liquor smuggling to the United States, where Prohibition still was in effect. This scandal caused members of Parliament to lose confidence in the governing Liberals.

▲ Arthur Meighen (1874-1960) was the leader of the Conservative Party during the 1925 general election campaign. The Conservatives won the most seats in the House of Commons, but they fell seven seats short of a majority. Meighen served as prime minister of Canada from July 1920 to December 1921 and from June to September 1926. The Liberals regained control of the government in the 1926 general election.

▼ An entry in Mackenzie King's diary on the day of the 1925 election reveals the prime minister's thoughts about the election results. Meighen's support for high protective tariffs that benefited Canadian industry won the Conservatives many votes in the Maritime Provinces and Ontario. The Conservatives fared worse in the West, where many people favored freer trade.

There can be no doubt that money lies at the basis of our whole defeat—money from the big interests—seeking further protection—and lack of organization on our part. . . . Protection . . . makes a very selfish appeal. Meighen did not hesitate to make it in every direction. . . . It looked at one a.m. as if he had within six of a majority—but not enough to be entitled to form a government till after prlt. [parliament] meets . . . It looks like a heavy road ahead, but the Progressives may come in with us . . . then if he [Meighen] wins in the H. of C. [House of Commons] it looks like another election or great uncertainty again for awhile. We must begin to build up an organization at once.

Mackenzie King, Oct. 29, 1929.

▶ The shoe of a liquor smuggler arrested at the Canada-U.S. border in 1924. The attached wooden blocks made the smuggler's footprints look like hoof-prints. Smuggling between Canada and the United States was a profitable business in the 1920's. In 1926, evidence came to light showing that Canadian customs officials had accepted bribes to overlook smuggling. This scandal led to a crisis of confidence in the Liberal government, which had been formed only with the support of the Progressives after the October 1925 general election.

A strong *censure* [criticism] of Hon. Jacques Bureau, former minister of customs, under whose administration the *degeneration* [worsening] of the Customs Department was "greatly accelerated," along with recommendations for sweeping reorganization of the customs service, the dismissal of various officials and the suspension of others, is made in the report of the customs investigating committee, presented to parliament this afternoon.

The report finds that Hon. Jacques Bureau, who was minister of customs till shortly before the general elections, "failed to appreciate and properly *discharge* [perform] the responsibilities of his office and as a result there was a lack of efficient, continuous and vigorous control of *subordinates* [underlings] by the headquarters staff at Ottawa."

The Ottawa Evening Citizen, 1926

◀ A newspaper story from *The Ottawa Evening Citizen* of June 18, 1926, reports that a parliamentary committee placed blame on Senator Jacques Bureau for allowing corruption to occur in the Customs Department. Bureau was minister of customs during a period when some customs officials cooperated with smugglers. Many people were angry that Prime Minister Mackenzie King made Bureau a senator following the customs scandal.

NOW YOU KNOW

- The Conservatives won the most seats, but not a majority, in the House of Commons in a 1925 general election.
- The Liberals formed a minority government with the support of the Progressives in Parliament.
- Corruption in the customs ministry damaged the Liberals' reputation not long after the election.

The King-Byng Affair

OWING TO THE PROBLEMS OF CORRUPTION IN THE GOVERNMENT, a confidence vote was to be held in Parliament in June 1926. House members would vote on whether the government was fit to continue. King hoped to avoid the likelihood of losing the vote. He asked Canada's governor general, Julian Hedworth George Byng (1862-1935), to *dissolve* (break up) Parliament and call an election. (The governor general represents Canada's head of state, the king or queen of Britain.) Byng refused King's request. King was surprised because the British government usually did not interfere in Canadian internal affairs. King resigned, and Byng asked Conservative leader Arthur Meighen to form a government. However, Parliament voted "no confidence" in Meighen's government in July, after Meighen overlooked certain rules regarding the appointment of government ministers. The Liberals were re-elected in September.

1

▶ A June 28, 1926, letter from Prime Minister Mackenzie King to Governor General Byng expressed King's feelings about Byng's refusal to dissolve Parliament. King complained that Byng had meddled in Canadian affairs and that Meighen, who seved as prime minister from June 29 to September 25, had gained that office "unconstitutionally."

◀ Governor General Byng in military dress in 1922. Byng, a British Army officer, became popular with Canadians because of his military leadership during World War I. However, many Canadians disagreed with his actions during the King-Byng affair.

2

As a refusal by a Governor-General to accept the advice of a Prime Minister is a serious step at any time, and most serious under existing conditions in all parts of the British Empire today, there will be raised, I fear, by the refusal on Your Excellency's part to accept the advice tendered a grave constitutional question without precedent [earlier instance] in the history of Great Britain for a century, and in the history of Canada since Confederation.

Prime Minister Mackenzie King, 1926

3

I have to await the verdict of history to prove my having adopted a wrong course, and this I do with an easy conscience that, right or wrong, I have acted in the interests of Canada and implicated no one else in my decision.

Governor General
Byng, 1926

◀ A letter from Governor General Byng to King George V of the United Kingdom expressed Byng's belief that he had done what was best for Canada when he refused to dissolve Parliament in June 1926.

4

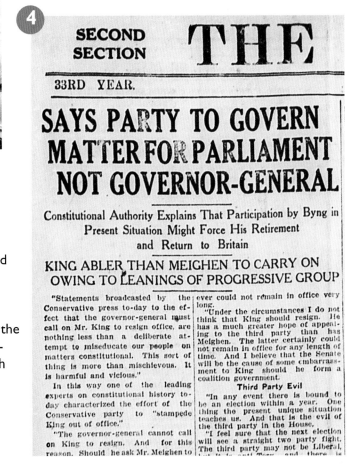

SECOND SECTION **THE**

33RD YEAR.

SAYS PARTY TO GOVERN MATTER FOR PARLIAMENT NOT GOVERNOR-GENERAL

Constitutional Authority Explains That Participation by Byng in Present Situation Might Force His Retirement and Return to Britain

KING ABLER THAN MEIGHEN TO CARRY ON OWING TO LEANINGS OF PROGRESSIVE GROUP

"Statements broadcasted by the Conservative press to-day to the effect that the governor-general must call on Mr. King to resign office, are nothing less than a deliberate attempt to miseducate our people on matters constitutional. This sort of thing is more than mischievous. It is harmful and vicious."

In this way one of the leading experts on constitutional history to-day characterized the effort of the Conservative party to "stampede King out of office."

"The governor-general cannot call on King to resign. And for this reason. Should he ask Mr. Meighen to

ever could not remain in office very long.

"Under the circumstances I do not think that King should resign. He has a much greater hope of appealing to the third party than has Meighen. The latter certainly could not remain in office for any length of time. And I believe that the Senate will be the cause of some embarrassment to King should he form a coalition government.

Third Party Evil

"In any event there is bound to be an election within a year. One thing the present unique situation teaches us. And that is the evil of the third party in the House.

"I feel sure that the next election will see a straight two party fight. The third party may not be Liberal,

▶ On Oct. 31, 1925, two days following a general election, *The Toronto Daily Star* printed an article editorializing that the Canadian Parliament, and not the governor general, should decide which party would govern Canada. The author of the article expresses the opinion, which existed even before the King-Byng affair, that Canadians rather than British representatives should control Canadian politics.

NOW YOU KNOW

- To avoid losing a confidence vote in 1926, Prime Minister Mackenzie King asked Governor General Byng to dissolve Parliament.
- Byng refused, King resigned, and Byng asked the Conservatives to form a government.
- Many Canadians viewed Byng's actions as an attack on their political independence.

Women's Rights

THE MOVEMENT FOR WOMEN'S RIGHTS gained support during World War I. The campaign for women's *suffrage* (the right to vote) was part of this movement. In January 1916, Manitoba became the first province to give women the right to vote in provincial elections. Saskatchewan and Alberta granted women provincial voting rights later in 1916. Most other provinces followed suit over the next few years. Quebec was the last province to grant women suffrage, in 1940. The Canada Elections Act of 1918 gave all Canadian women over the age of 21 the right to vote in federal elections, whether or not they were allowed to vote in provincial elections at that time.

◀ A sign posted by the Canadian Pacific Railway Company in 1913 in Cockspur Street, London, England, warned *suffragettes* that they were not welcome in Canada. Suffragettes were women who fought for women's right to vote.

▶ An office-management handbook published in 1925 explained why it was better to hire women than men for secretarial jobs. This author expressed the idea that women in general had less professional ambition than men. In reality, society had not given women much of an opportunity to develop careers outside the home. Many people believed that men and women should have different, clearly defined roles in society.

A woman is to be preferred for the secretarial position for she is not *averse to* [against] doing minor tasks, work involving the handling of petty details, which would irk and irritate ambitious young men, who usually feel that the work they are doing is of no importance if it can be performed by some person with a lower salary. Most such men are also anxious to get ahead and to be promoted from position to position, and consequently if there is much work of a detail[ed] character to be done, and they are expected to perform it, they will not remain satisfied and will probably seek a position elsewhere.

William H. Leffingwell, *Office Management, Principles and Practice*, 1925

3

▶ In a speech from the 1920's, Agnes Macphail expressed her desire for complete equality between men and women. Unlike Macphail and other supporters of women's rights, some people believed that the role of women should be limited to that of homemaker.

I do not want to be the angel of any home; I want for myself what I want for other women, absolute equality. After that is secured then men and women can take turns at being angels.

Agnes Macphail

4

◀ Before entering politics, Agnes Campbell Macphail (1890-1954) worked as a teacher. On Dec. 6, 1921, Macphail became the first woman elected to the Canadian House of Commons. The 1921 general election in Canada was the first in which Canadian women were allowed to vote. Macphail served in the federal Parliament until 1940. Later, she became a member of Ontario's provincial legislature.

NOW YOU KNOW

- The Prairie Provinces were the first provinces to grant women suffrage, in 1916.
- In 1918, Canadian women gained the right to vote in federal elections.
- Agnes Macphail, elected in 1921, was the first female member of the Canadian House of Commons.

The Persons Case

IN 1929, FIVE WOMEN FROM ALBERTA ACHIEVED AN IMPORTANT LEGAL VICTORY. The women, called the Famous Five, were social reformers. In 1927, they asked the Supreme Court of Canada to examine the meaning of the word "persons" in the British North America Act to determine whether it included women. On April 24, 1928, the Supreme Court decided women were not "persons" and so could not be appointed to Canada's Senate. The Famous Five appealed to the Judicial Committee of Britain's Privy Council, the highest court of appeal for Canada. On October 18, 1929, the Committee concluded that "the word 'persons' included both the male and female sex."

▲ Nellie McClung (1873-1951), *left*, and Emily Murphy (1868-1933), *right*, were two of the activists known as the Famous Five. Alice Jamieson, *center*, was a women's rights supporter from Alberta. Jamieson and Murphy became two of Canada's first female judges. The victory of the Famous Five in the Persons Case led to greater opportunities for, and increased participation by, women in public life. Their appeal to Britain's Privy Council highlighted the fact that the United Kingdom still controlled some areas of Canadian government.

2

▶ A letter from Emily Murphy to the other members of the Famous Five—Henrietta Muir Edwards (1849-1931), Louise McKinney (1868-193), Irene Parlby (1868-1965), and Nellie McClung—expresses optimism about their chance of winning the Persons Case. Although she wrote this letter after Canada's Supreme Court had ruled that the word "persons" in the British North America Act referred only to men, Murphy planned to appeal the British Privy Council, whose decision could overrule that of the Supreme Court.

For the several years past the women of Canada, owing to what appeared to be a hopeless situation, took comparitively [sic] little interest in this matter of the interpretation of the word 'Persons' in Section 24 of the B. N. A. [British North America] Act. Our action in appealing to the Supreme Court of Canada for a ruling gave to the women of all parties a renewed hope and had the effect of stimulating them to something approaching definite action. We have every reason to felicitate [congratulate] ourselves in this behalf.

Of the ultimate results I have not the slightest doubt. Nothing can prevent our winning.

Emily Murphy, May 1928

3

The hand that rocks the cradle does not rule the world. If it did . . . the world would be a sweeter, cleaner, safer place than it is now!

Nellie McClung, 1915

◀ In her 1915 book, *In Times Like These*, Nellie McClung argued that the world would be better if women had a hand in government. The quote is a response to a common saying about mothers: "The hand that rocks the cradle rules the world."

NOW YOU KNOW

- In 1927, the Famous Five asked the Supreme Court of Canada to examine the meaning of "persons" in the British North America Act.

- In 1928, the Supreme Court ruled that "persons" did not include women, and so women could not serve in the Senate.

- In 1929, the Judicial Committee of Britain's Privy Council overruled the Supreme Court and decided that "persons" did include women.

First Nations

FIRST NATIONS PEOPLE (NATIVE PEOPLE, ALSO CALLED INDIANS) IN CANADA continued to be treated as second-class citizens during the 1920's. They were made to live on reserves, deprived of their traditional hunting grounds, and discouraged from speaking their native languages. Many died from disease and a poor diet. The Dominion government wanted to *assimilate* (incorporate) First Nations people into mainstream European Canadian society. Many First Nations children were sent to residential schools where a nonnative lifestyle was forced upon them. American Indians in the United States gained the right to vote in 1924, but Canada's First Nations were not granted this right until 1960.

1

I want to get rid of the Indian problem. . . . Our object is to continue until there is not a single Indian in Canada that has not been absorbed into the body politic, and there is no Indian question, and no Indian Department . . .

Duncan Campbell Scott, 1920

◀ In 1920, Duncan Campbell Scott (1862-1947), deputy superintendent of the Canadian Department of Indian Affairs, appeared before members of the House of Commons to defend a bill that would force First Nations people to become *enfranchised*. Enfranchised Indians gained the right to vote and other privileges held by non-Indians. But they lost their legal rights as Indians and their right to live on a reserve. Before 1920, enfranchisement was voluntary. A policy of forced enfranchisement was in effect from 1920 to 1922 and from 1933 to 1951.

▶ Thomas L., a First Nations man, writes in a 1925 letter to Charles Cooke a request to become enfranchised. Cooke was an official at Canada's Department of Indian Affairs. The request was somewhat unusual as relatively few Indians voluntarily chose to become enfranchised. Many First Nations people saw enfranchisement as a threat to their traditional way of life and their tribal identity. First Nations women who married nonnative men automatically became enfranchised and lost their legal status as Indians, defined by the Indian Act of 1876.

2

Now Charlie, you know me pretty well. I am always amongst the white people and making an honest living and I have a good reputation among the white people. And tell the Department that I fought for my country for Freedom. And now all I am asking the Department is to grant me our enfranchisement. I need the money and I would like to have [it] as soon as possible. I am ambitious and I believe in an Education.

Thomas L., November 16, 1925

▲ First Nations people on a reserve in Saskatchewan, 1926. The British government began confining First Nations people in Canada to reserves in the 1800's. After the Dominion of Canada was created in 1867, the Canadian government continued this policy. People who met the legal definition of Indians—known as status Indians—did not have to pay taxes on reserve property. However, they were denied many civil rights held by Canadian citizens.

NOW YOU KNOW

- In the early 1900's, First Nations people lacked many civil rights held by nonnative Canadians.
- Canada's government sought to incorporate all First Nations people into mainstream Canadian society.
- The government encouraged First Nations people to give up their legal Indian status voluntarily and become Canadian citizens, a process called enfranchisement.

Immigration

M ORE THAN 6 MILLION PEOPLE IMMIGRATED TO CANADA FROM 1850 to 1930. They included people from the United States, Europe, and Asia who brought their own beliefs and customs to their new home. During economic downturns, the Canadian government limited immigration because immigrants often were blamed for rising unemployment. In more prosperous times, however, the government and businesses encouraged immigration because of the need for labor. In the 1920's, Canadian railroad companies were in such a hurry to find laborers that they recruited workers in Europe and transported them to Canada without following proper legal procedures. High unemployment at the end of the decade ended the practice.

▶ A Chinese man washes gold in the Fraser River in British Columbia in 1875. Canada's government encouraged Chinese workers to immigrate to Canada in the late 1800's to help build the Canadian Pacific Railway. After the railroad's completion in 1885, the government tried to discourage Chinese immigration by heavily taxing Chinese immigrants. The Chinese Immigration Act barred nearly all Chinese from Canada from 1923 to 1947.

Canada has been increasingly careful about the kind of immigrants permitted to enter the country, and the regulations are in some respects more *stringent* [strict] than those of the United States. Physical and mental defectives, professional *agitators* [those who stir up discontent] and enemy *aliens* [foreigners] are not admitted. All males under eighteen years of age, excepting farm laborers and domestic servants, must have $250.

from *The World Book Encyclopedia Annual for 1922*

◀ The World Book Encyclopedia Annual for 1922 describes immigration restrictions in 1920's Canada. In 1920, Canada's government passed legislation requiring mechanics, artisans, and laborers immigrating to Canada to have at least $250 and transportation to their place of destination. The legislation was intended to limit immigration during a period of high unemployment that followed World War I.

▲ Russian Christians called Doukhobors work on a group farm in British Columbia in the 1910's. More than 7,000 Doukhobors immigrated from Russia to western Canada in 1899. The Doukhobors adopted many ideas of the Russian author Leo Tolstoy. They believed that the "voice within" each person was his or her guide and that priests, churches, and governments were unnecessary.

▶ A boy talks to his father in John Marlyn's novel *Under the Ribs of Death*. First published in 1957, the book is a tale of poor immigrant life in Winnipeg in the 1920's. Immigrants of British descent generally had an advantage over other immigrants in Canada.

"The English," he whispered. "Pa, the only people who count are the English. Their fathers got all the best jobs. They're the only ones nobody calls foreigners. Nobody ever makes fun of their names or calls them 'bologny-eaters' or laughs at the way they dress or talk. . . . 'cause when you're English it's the same as bein' Canadian."

John Marlyn

NOW YOU KNOW

• Millions of people immigrated to Canada in the late 1800's and early 1900's.

• Early Canadian immigration laws were closely tied to the national economy.

• The Chinese Immigration Act banned nearly all Chinese from migrating to Canada from 1923 to 1947.

Art By and About Canadians

DURING THE 1920'S, CANADIAN ARTISTS AND WRITERS began to create a distinctly Canadian body of art and literature. The Group of Seven, a school of Canadian landscape painters from Toronto, Ontario, held its first exhibition in 1920. The group became a dominant force in Canadian art in the 1920's and 1930's. Canadian poets such as Abraham Moses Klein (1909-1972), Francis Reginald Scott (1899-1985), and Arthur James Marshall Smith (1902-1980) helped to create a national literature for their country. During this period, foreigners also produced artwork about Canada. For example, American filmmaker Robert Flaherty (1884-1951) made the documentary *Nanook of the North* (1922) about Canada's native Inuit people.

◀ Postage stamps featuring paintings by the Group of Seven. The landscape of northern Canada inspired the group's art, which featured brilliant colors and free brush strokes. The original group included Franklin Carmichael (1890-1945), Lawren Harris (1885-1970), A. Y. Jackson (1882-1974), Franz Johnston (1888-1949), Arthur Lismer (1885-1969), J. E. H. MacDonald (1873-1932), and Frederick H. Varley (1881-1969).

▶ *Pens and Pirates,* a 1923 book by the Canadian literary critic and editor William Arthur Deacon (1890-1977), voices the desire for a distinct Canadian literature. Deacon and others believed that the influence of the United Kingdom and the United States stifled true Canadian forms of expression.

Our struggle for nationhood needs writers and national magazines with native force behind them, filled with Canadian thought from the gifted Canadian pens which we drive out each year. "Moulders of public opinion" is a phrase I hate. It indicates bulldozing on the part of the press. Yet, in a less offensive way, they are what we need—men who will take the *nebulous* [hazy] ideas and vague stirrings of emotion and "mould" them into *concise* [brief but meaningful] and beautiful forms . . .

W. A. Deacon, 1923

3

The exhibition is a most stimulating one . . . the younger and "modern" artists of the Dominion are strongly represented. Their work will cause a good deal of discussion, not all amiable. . . . But they are native and interpret the country as no other art medium has yet been able to. Their originality of style, their forceful colors and masses and their unorthodox methods single them out as a genuine national expression, and if one cannot always sympathize with the outlook or appreciate the ability of the artists, one must admit that they are significant and speak definitely in terms of those they represent.

The Ottawa Citizen, 1927

◀ A newspaper article in *The Ottawa Citizen* of Jan. 12, 1927, describes the second annual exhibition of contemporary Canadian art at the National Gallery of Canada in Ottawa, Ontario. The exhibition included paintings by members of the Group of Seven and by a number of artists from Ottawa.

4

▶ The motion-picture masterpiece documentary *Nanook of the North* (1922), by filmmaker Robert Flaherty, captured the hardship of Inuit life in Arctic Quebec. The ancestors of the Inuit people began to spread eastward from what is now Alaska and the area around the Bering Sea from about A.D. 1000. Traditional Inuit life in Canada changed significantly beginning in the 1950's with the decline of the fur trade and a decrease in the population of caribou, which the Inuit hunted.

NOW YOU KNOW

- A distinctly Canadian body of art developed in the early 1900's.
- The Group of Seven was an important force in Canadian art in the 1920's and 1930's.
- Many Canadians felt that their emerging sense of nationhood needed to be reflected in art and literature that were distinctly Canadian.

Inventions and Discoveries

CANADIANS WERE RESPONSIBLE FOR A NUMBER OF HIGHLY SIGNIFICANT inventions and discoveries in the 1920's and 1930's. In 1921 and 1922, four researchers at the University of Toronto isolated and prepared the hormone insulin for treating the disease diabetes. Their work revolutionized the treatment of diabetes. The development of Pablum, an infant cereal product enriched with vitamins and minerals, by Canadian pediatricians in 1930 helped prevent many children from becoming malnourished and getting the bone disease called rickets. Other scientific accomplishments by Canadians in the early 1900's included the invention of the alternating-current radio tube.

1

Insulin is not a cure for diabetes; it is a treatment. It enables the diabetic to burn sufficient carbohydrates, so that proteins and fats may be added to the diet in sufficient quantities to provide energy for the economic burdens of life.

Frederick Banting, 1925

◀ Canadian surgeon Frederick Grant Banting (1891-1941) describes the medical use of insulin in a Nobel Lecture delivered on Sept. 15, 1925. Insulin is a hormone, made in the pancreas, that regulates the body's use of sugars and other nutrients. People with diabetes do not make enough insulin on their own. The team that isolated and prepared insulin included Banting, Canadian physiologist Charles Herbert Best (1899-1978), Canadian biochemist James Bertram Collip (1892-1965), and Scottish physiologist John James Rickard Macleod. Banting and Macleod won a 1923 Nobel Prize for the discovery.

2

▶ Charles Best (left) and Frederick Banting pose for a 1921 photo on the roof of the University of Toronto Medical Building with the first dog to be kept alive by insulin. Before insulin was given to humans, dogs were used in experiments to isolate the hormone. The first patient with diabetes was treated on Jan. 11, 1922. Banting and Best chose not to patent their discovery, which would have given them the sole right to produce insulin and make money from it. Instead, they allowed the University of Toronto to make insulin readily available to anyone who needed it.

3

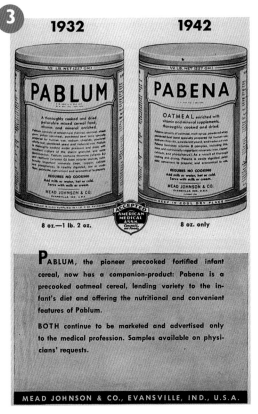

1932   **1942**

▲ A 1943 advertisement by Mead Johnson & Co. promotes Pablum cereal and its new companion product, Pabena. The ad bears the seal of approval of the American Medical Association and offers samples to physicians. A team including pediatricians Frederick Tisdall (1893-1949), Theodore Drake (1891-1959), and Alan Brown (1887-1960) of the Hospital for Sick Children in Toronto developed Pablum, which became available in 1931.

▼ A postage stamp honors the 1925 invention of the alternating-current radio tube by Canadian broadcaster and inventor Edward Samuel Rogers (1900-1939). Radios with alternating-current tubes could run on ordinary household electric power. Before Rogers' invention, radios required battery power.

4

NOW YOU KNOW

- Scientists in Canada emerged onto the world stage when in 1921 they isolated and prepared insulin to treat diabetes.
- In 1925, Edward Rogers invented the alternating-current radio tube.
- The development of Pablum cereal by Canadian doctors improved children's nutrition in the 1930's.

Balfour Declaration of 1926

THE LIBERALS WON CONTROL OF CANADA'S GOVERNMENT in a September 1926 election and Mackenzie King again became prime minister. In October, King attended the Imperial Conference in London, where he fought for full Canadian self-government. The conference produced the Balfour Declaration of 1926, also called the Balfour Report. The report acknowledged the growing diplomatic and political independence shown by Canada since World War I and by other dominion countries. The report was named for Sir Arthur James Balfour, Earl of Balfour (1848-1930), the British diplomat and former prime minister who drafted it.

▲ Canadian delegates to the Imperial Conference in London in October 1926, from left to right: Minister of Justice Ernest Lapointe (1876-1941); Prime Minister Mackenzie King; industrialist and politician Vincent Massey (1887-1967); and High Commissioner to the United Kingdom Peter Larkin (1856-1930). The conference established basic principles to guide relations among the Commonwealth nations— that is, the United Kingdom and its increasingly independent dominions.

2

They are autonomous Communities within the British Empire, equal in status, in no way *subordinate* [subject] one to another in any aspect of their domestic or external affairs, though united by a common allegiance to the Crown, and freely associated as members of the British Commonwealth of Nations.

from the Balfour Declaration of 1926

◀ The Balfour Declaration of 1926, also known as the Balfour Report, defined the dominion countries of the United Kingdom as constitutionally equal to the United Kingdom and to one another. Previously, the dominions largely had controlled their own domestic affairs, but not their foreign affairs. The declaration became law in 1931.

▶ The United Kingdom article in *The World Book Encyclopedia Annual for 1926* contrasted the quiet, steady nature of the dominions' development as independent nations with the considerable importance of their achievement. The Imperial Conference declared Canada and other dominions of the British Empire to be completely self-governing countries.

3

The Dominions began more and more to act on their own initiative in matters which theretofore had been held to be sole *prerogatives* [rights] of the government of the Empire, though not in a spirit which was *antagonistic to* [opposing] the mother country. They have without blare of trumpets been making themselves free, taking their destinies into their own hands. The action of the Imperial Conference placed the seal of approval on the ambitions of the Dominions, and the momentous thing was accomplished as quietly and with as little *ostentation* [showiness] as though a minor ruling were involved, and not one destined to influence a large part of the world.

from *The World Book Encyclopedia Annual for 1926*

NOW YOU KNOW

- The Liberal Party won control of Canada's government again in September 1926.
- British and dominion representatives attended the Imperial Conference of 1926, which resulted in the Balfour Declaration, also called the Balfour Report.
- The Balfour Report redefined dominions of the British Empire as fully self-governing nations.

The Great Depression

THE GREAT DEPRESSION BEGAN IN 1929 with the stock market crash in the United States and spread throughout the world. The stock market crash occurred in October 1929, when the price of shares on the New York Stock Exchange fell rapidly. Panicked investors rushed to sell their shares and lost huge sums of money. The Depression caused a sharp drop in foreign trade. It especially hurt worldwide demand for Canadian food products, lumber, and minerals. The decline in export income forced thousands of Canadian factories and stores, plus many coal mines, to close. Hundreds of thousands of Canadians lost their jobs and homes, and millions were forced to depend on charity to survive. A rapid fall in grain prices and a severe drought worsened the Depression in the Prairie Provinces.

1

Looking farther and into the long future, it is not too much to expect that an *unprecedented* [never known before] period of prosperity lies ahead.

S. J. Moore, 1929

◀ In his annual report to shareholders, Bank of Nova Scotia President S. J. Moore predicted boom times ahead. Developments proved Moore completely wrong. The stock market crash of 1929 plunged economies around the world into depression. Other countries could no longer afford to buy Canadian minerals, timber, and wheat. Some experts believe that reckless borrowing and a lack of regulation of the banking sector helped to cause the stock market crash.

▼ Unemployed people wait in line to apply for a job at a department store in Edmonton, Alberta, in 1931. By 1933, about one-fourth of Canada's workforce was unemployed. Thousands of farm families were on the brink of starvation.

2

3

In the old days we could send people from the cities to the country. If they went out today they would meet another army of unemployed coming back from the country to the city; that outlet is closed. What can these people do? They have been driven from our parks; they have been driven from our streets; they have been driven from our buildings and in this city [Ottawa] they actually took refuge on the garbage heaps.

J. S. Woodsworth, 1931

◀ Speaking in the House of Commons, labor politician J. S. Woodsworth described the desperation that characterized the Great Depression. Unemployment and poverty were problems in rural as well as urban areas. Severe droughts that destroyed crops for several years in a row worsened the suffering of farmers. Dry topsoil blew away, and grasshoppers ate what little was left of ruined crops. These conditions forced more than 200,000 Canadians off the land.

4

▶ Strikers from unemployment relief camps ride a train bound for Ottawa in 1935. The "On to Ottawa Trek" began in June, when strikers from British Columbia boarded freight trains headed east. They planned to travel to Ottawa to demand better conditions for the unemployed. However, the trek ended in July in Regina, Saskatchewan, where government officials stopped the trekkers and a riot involving local police and the Royal Canadian Mounted Police occurred.

NOW YOU KNOW

- The stock market crash in the United States in October 1929 marked the start of the Great Depression.
- The Depression lowered the demand for Canadian exports.
- Many Canadians lost their farms, homes, jobs, and savings.

Poverty and Politics

THE UNEMPLOYED RELIED ON SOUP KITCHENS AND FOOD BANKS TO SURVIVE the Depression. At the time, there were no unemployment insurance, welfare payments, medical care, or job-creation programs. Prime Minister Mackenzie King insisted the provinces were responsible for helping unemployed people. Labor politicians Abraham Albert Heaps (1885-1954) and J. S. Woodsworth argued for the introduction of an insurance plan that would pay money to people when they were jobless. The Conservatives accused the Liberal government of being corrupt and uncaring. In the federal election of July 28, 1930, the Conservatives won a majority of seats in Parliament and Richard Bedford Bennett (1870-1947) became prime minister.

▶ In an address to the House of Commons in 1930, Prime Minsister Mackenzie King expressed his unwillingness to help Conservative provincial governments pay for unemployment relief. The Conservatives held up King's remark as proof that the Liberal government was uncaring and out of touch with Canadians' suffering. During the same address, King said that he might consider giving federal money to provincial provinces with Progressive leaders to help them handle the unemployment crisis.

1

With respect to giving moneys out of the federal treasury to any Tory [Conservative] government in this country for these alleged unemployment puposes, with these governments situated as they are today, with policies diametrically [directly] opposed to those of this government, I would not give them a five cent piece.
Mackenzie King, 1930

▼ A billboard in Calgary, Alberta, urges voters to support Richard Bedford Bennett and the Conservative Party in the 1930 federal election. Bennett, himself a millionaire, promised to lead Canada out of the Depression or "perish in the attempt." Bennett's government spent much more on relief than was spent in the previous decade to help the unemployed.

2

▶ Writing in 1938, Dorothy King, director of the Montreal School of Social Work from 1933 to 1950, describes the difficulty of obtaining financial aid during the Great Depression. Many people lost all that they owned, went into debt, and were forced to leave their homes before they could obtain unemployment aid.

3

In the early days of the depression, the difficulties of securing aid and its frequent inadequacy were responsible for cases of acute suffering and the breakdown of morale. Many of the unemployed sold their homes and other possessions, ran into debt till their credit was exhausted, and endured serious privations [wants] before reaching the unemployed aid lists. In many areas no rent was paid and evictions were common.

Dorothy King, 1938

4

◀ Homeless men known as hobos build a road in British Columbia in May 1934, during the Great Depression. Unemployed workers began *riding the rods*—that is, boarding trains illegally and traveling from place to place in search of work. Riding the rods was dangerous and sometimes deadly. Some hobos rode on actual rods underneath the train cars when the cars were locked and they could not get inside them.

NOW YOU KNOW

- Prime Minister Mackenzie King argued that provincial governments, rather than the federal government, should help unemployed people during the Great Depression.
- Labor politicians supported the introduction of unemployment insurance.
- The Conservative Party portrayed the Liberal government as uncaring and won the 1930 federal election.

The Statute of Westminster

B Y THE START OF THE 1930'S, Canada had strengthened its relationship with the United States and entered into an agreement that said Canada was equal in status to Britain. Canadians' sense of national identity was much stronger than it had been before World War I. Canadian embassies had been established in Washington, D.C.; Paris; and Tokyo by the end of the 1920's. Political developments caused Canadians to focus on what united them rather than what divided them. In 1931, the Parliament of the United Kindom ratified the Statute of Westminster. This *statute* (law) legalized the declaration, made in the Balfour Report, that the dominions were independent countries.

Section 3 [Power of Parliament of Dominion to legislate extra-territorially]
It is hereby declared and enacted that the Parliament of a Dominion has full power to make laws having *extra-territorial* [outside Canada] operation.

Section 4 [Parliament of United Kingdom not to legislate for Dominion except by its consent]
No Act of Parliament of the United Kingdom passed after the *commencement* [introduction] of this Act shall extend or be deemed to extend, to a Dominion as part of the law of that Dominion, unless it is expressly declared in that Act that that Dominion has requested, and consented to, the enactment thereof.

Section 11 [Meaning of "Colony" in future Acts]
Notwithstanding anything in the Interpretation Act, 1889, the expression "Colony" shall not, in any Act of the Parliament of the United Kingdom passed after the commencement of this Act, include a Dominion or any Province or State forming a part of a Dominion.

from the Statute of Westminster, 1931

▲ The Statute of Westminster established the legal framework for the Commonwealth of Nations, a new association of independent countries formerly under British control. This law gave the dominions of the British Empire independence in all areas except those in which they chose to remain subject to the United Kingdom. For example, Canada's federal and provincial governments decided that changes to Canada's constitution would remain subject to British approval, an arrangement which lasted until 1982.

2 The year saw the formal abolition of the last *vestige* [trace] of legal inequality between the governments and parliaments of the dominions of the British Commonwealth, and the government and Parliament of Great Britain. By what is named the Statute of Westminster, which was passed by large majorities in both Houses and received the assent of the King on December 11, the British Parliament explicitly renounced the right—long *obsolete* [outdated]—to legislate on dominion affairs, except at the request of the dominions concerned; and recognized that legislation passed by dominion parliaments has the same validity as that passed by the British Parliament.

from *The World Book Encyclopedia Annual for 1931*

◀ The "United Kingdom" article in *The World Book Encyclopedia Annual for 1931* commented on the passage of the Statute of Westminster and expressed a general hope for equality within the new Commonwealth of Nations. The original Commonwealth members were Australia, the United Kingdom, Canada, the Irish Free State (Ireland), New Zealand, Newfoundland, and South Africa. Today, the Commonwealth includes about 50 independent countries and about 25 *dependencies* (areas that do not have complete self-government).

▶ Queen Elizabeth II of the United Kingdom (1926-   ) and Canadian Prime Minister Pierre Trudeau (1919-2000) sign the Constitution Act of 1982. This act eliminated the need for British approval of Canadian constitutional amendments. The revised constitution took effect on April 17, 1982. It replaced the British North America Act as the basic governing document of Canada.

NOW YOU KNOW

- By the beginning of the 1930's, Canada had developed a strong sense of national identity.
- In 1931, the British Parliament passed the Statute of Westminster, a law granting independence to the dominions of the United Kingdom.
- Canada's national and provincial leaders initially chose not to adopt full authority over the Canadian constitution until 1982.

Timeline

August 1914-November 1918	About 60,000 Canadian soldiers lose their lives in World War I
January 1916	Women gain the vote in Manitoba.
March 1916	Women gain the vote in Saskatchewan.
April 1916	Women gain the vote in Alberta.
April 14, 1917	Canadian troops take Vimy Ridge from the Germans during the Battle of Vimy Ridge.
1917	Resolution IX of the Imperial War Cabinet recognizes Canada and the other British dominions as autonomous nations of an imperial commonwealth.
Aug. 29, 1917	The Military Service Act takes effect, introducing conscription in Canada.
Dec. 6, 1917	The port of Halifax, Nova Scotia, is devastated when a French ship carrying explosives collides with a Norwegian ship on its way to pick up relief supplies; more than 2,000 people are killed in the explosion.
Dec. 17, 1917	The Unionists, who support military conscription, win the federal election.
May 15-June 25, 1919	The Winnipeg General Strike closes factories, halts trade, and stops train service in Winnipeg, Manitoba.
1919	In response to the Winnipeg strike, the government invokes the War Measures Act of 1914 to restrict the activities of labor unions and the radical press.
June 28, 1919	Canada signs the Treaty of Versailles, the World War I peace settlement.
1920	The Group of Seven holds its first exhibition in Toronto.
Jan. 10, 1920	Canada becomes a member of the League of Nations.
Dec. 6, 1921	The Liberal Party wins the federal election and William Lyon Mackenzie King becomes prime minister.
Dec. 6, 1921	Agnes Macphail becomes the first woman elected to Canada's House of Commons.
1921	Leaders of the dominions of the British Empire meet at the Imperial Conference in London.
1921-1922	Researchers at the University of Toronto isolate and prepare insulin to treat patients with diabetes.
September 1922	Prime Minister Mackenzie King refuses to help the British hold the Turkish town of Chanak.
1923	The Chinese Immigration Act bans virtually all Chinese immigration to Canada.
March 2, 1923	Canada signs the Halibut Treaty with the United States.
Oct. 1-Nov. 8, 1923	Prime Minister Mackenzie King represents Canada at the Imperial Conference in London.
Oct. 29, 1925	Following a federal election, Mackenzie King's Liberals form a minority government.
June 1926	The King-Byng affair strains Canada's relations with the United Kingdom.
Sept. 14, 1926	The Liberals win a federal election and Mackenzie King becomes prime minister again.
October-November 1926	The Imperial Conference produces the Balfour Declaration, which establishes the principle that all the British dominions are equal and not subordinate to the United Kingdom.
1927	The Canadian government presents the first federal old-age pension check.
1928	Canadian farmers produce their largest wheat harvest on record.
Oct. 18, 1929	The Judicial Committee of Britain's Privy Council rules that the word "persons" in the British North America Act includes women.
October 1929	The stock market crash in the United States marks the beginning of the Great Depression.
July 28, 1930	The Conservative Party wins a federal election and Richard Bennett becomes prime minister.
Dec. 11, 1931	The Statute of Westminster, a British law, grants Canada and the other dominions full legal freedom, except in areas where the dominions choose to remain subordinate.

Sources

4-5 Document 2 – McCrae, John. *In Flanders Fields, and Other Poems.* New York: Thomas Y. Crowell Co., 1919. *Project Gutenberg.* Web. 14 May 2010. Document 3 – James, Ewin L. "Allies' Dictation to League Menaces French Cabinet." *New York Times* 9 Dec. 1920: 1+. Microfilm.

6-7 Document 2 – Borden, Robert. Letter to Sir George Perley. 4 Jan. 1916. In *World War I: Encyclopedia.* Ed. Spencer C. Tucker. Santa Barbara, CA: ABC-CLIO, 2005. Print. Document 3 – "Back in Time: Canada (1922)." *World Book Student.* Chicago, 2010. Web. 14 May 2010.

8-9 Document 2 – Report by the Methodist Church of Canada. Quoted in Hopkins, J. Castell. *The Canadian Annual Review of Public Affairs.* Toronto: The Canadian Review Co., 1919. *Google Books.* Web. 17 May 2010. Document 3 – Constitution and Laws of the One Big Union. 1919. Quoted in Savage, Marion Dutton. *Industrial Unionism in America.* New York: Ronald Press Co., 1922. *Google Books.* Web. 14 May 2010.

10-11 Document 2 – "Winnipeg Sees General Strike in Full Effect." *Gazette* [Montreal] 16 May 1919: 1+. *Google News.* Web. 19 May 2010. Document 4 – Canada. Department of Labor. *Labour Legislation in Canada as Existing December 31, 1928.* Ottawa: F. A. Acland, 1929. Print.

12-13 Document 2 – Coats, Robert Hamilton. Quoted in Thompson, John H., and Allen Seager. *Canada, 1922–1939: Decades of Discord.* Toronto: McClelland and Stewart, 1985. Print. Document 3 – "Back in Time: Canada (1922)." *World Book Student.* Chicago, 2010. Web. 14 May 2010.

14-15 Documents 2 – The Francoeur Resolution of 1918. Quoted in Hopkins, J. Castell. *The Canadian Annual Review of Public Affairs.* Toronto: The Canadian Review Co., 1919. *Google Books.* Web. 14 May 2010. Document 3 – Bourassa, Henri. 1918. Quoted in Finlay, John L., and Douglas N. Sprague. *The Structure of Canadian History.* 6th ed. Scarborough, Ont.: Prentice Hall, 2000. Print.

16-17 Document 2 – Crerar, Thomas. 1920. Quoted in Finlay, John L., and Douglas N. Sprague. *The Structure of Canadian History.* 6th ed. Scarborough, Ont.: Prentice Hall, 2000. Print. Document 3 – *The Canadian Forum* 1.1 (1920): 3-4. *Internet Archive.* Web. 14 May 2010.

18-19 Document 2 – Moore, Tom. 1925. Quoted in Thompson, John H., and Allen Seager. *Canada, 1922–1939: Decades of Discord.* Toronto: McClelland and Stewart, 1985. Print. Document 3– "Ask Federal Aid to Stop Moonshiners." *Calgary Daily Herald* 27 Jan. 1927: 1. Print.

20-21 Document 1 – Draft of the Constitution of the Farmer Union of Canada. 1922. Quoted in *Historical Essays on the Prairie Provinces.* Comp. Donald Swainson. Toronto: McClelland and Stewart, 1970. Print. Document 4 – *The Progressive* [newspaper]. 3 July 1924. Quoted in *Historical Essays on the Prairie Provinces.* Comp. Donald Swainson. Toronto: McClelland and Stewart, 1970. Print.

22-23 Document 2 – "Back in Time: Canada (1928)." *World Book Student.* Chicago, 2010. Web. 14 May 2010. Document 4 – Alberta Natural Resources Act, 1930. In *British North America Acts and Selected Statutes, 1867-1962.* Comp. Maurice Ollivier. Ottawa: Roger Duhamel, 1962. Print.

24-25 Document 2 – Cunningham, Louis A. *This Thing Called Love.* New York: L. Carrier, 1929. Print. Document 4 – Connors, Lewis. Open letter directed against Canada's financial institutions. June 1924. Quoted in Nerbas, Don. "Adapting to Decline: The Changing Business World of the Bourgeoisie in Saint John, NB, in the 1920's." *Canadian Historical Review* 89. 2 (2008): 151-87. Print.

26-27 Document 1 – "Back in Time: Canada (1929)." *World Book Student.* Chicago, 2010. Web. 14 May 2010. Document 3 – Stewart, J. L. "Canada's Motor Car Industry." *Canadian Geographical Journal* 14.4 (1937): 723. Print.

28-29 Document 2 – Harding, Warren G. Speech in Vancouver. July 1923. Quoted in Chapple, Joe M. *Life and Times of Warren G. Harding: Our After-War President.* Boston: Chapple Pub. Co., 1924. Print.

30-31 Document 2 – Woodsworth, J. S. Excerpts from two articles in the 18 July 1919 and 25 July 1919 issues of *Western Labor News.* Quoted in McNaught, Kenneth. *A Prophet in Politics: a Biography of J. S. Woodsworth.*

University of Toronto, 1959. Print. Document 3 – Mosher, Aaron R. Speech to the All-Canadian Congress of Labour. Nov. 1929. Quoted in Francis, R. D., Richard Jones, and Donald B. Smith. *Destinies: Canadian History Since Confederation.* Toronto: Holt, Rinehart, and Winston, 1988. Print.

32-33 Document 1 – King, Mackenzie. Diary entry. Fall 1922. Quoted in McNaught, Kenneth W. *The Pelican History of Canada.* New York: Penguin, 1988. Print. Document 2 – Meighen, Arthur. Speech in Toronto. 22 Sept. 1922. Quoted in Hopkins, J. Castell. *The Canadian Annual Review of Public Affairs.* Toronto: Canadian Review Co., 1923. Print.

34-35 Document 1 – King, William Lyon Mackenzie. Diary entry for 29 Oct. 1925. *Library and Archives Canada.* Web. 28 Apr. 2010. Document 4 – "Customs Report Censures Senator Bureau." *Ottawa Evening Citizen* 18 June 1926: 1-2. *Google News.* Web. 27 May 2010.

36-37 Document 2 – King, Mackenzie. Letter to Governor General Byng. 28 June 1926. In Hopkins, J. Castell. *The Canadian Annual Review of Public Affairs.* Toronto: Canadian Review Co., 1927. Print. Document 3 – Byng, Governor General. Letter to Mr. L. S. Amery. 30 June 1926. In *Historical Documents of Canada.* Ed. C. P. Stacey. Vol. 5. Toronto: Macmillan, 1972. Print.

38-39 Document 2 – Leffingwell, William H. *Office Management: Principles and Practice.* New York: A. W. Shaw, 1925. Print. Document 3 – Macphail, Agnes. Speech in the House of Commons. 26 Feb. 1925. Quoted in *Our Canada.* Ed. Leo Heaps. Toronto: J. Lorimer, 1991. Print.

40-41 Document 2 – Murphy, Emily. Letter to her four co-petitioners. May 1928. *Canadian Museum for Human Rights.* Web. 14 May 2010. Document 3 – McClung, Nellie L. *In Times Like These.* New York: D. Appleton, 1915. *Google Books.* Web. 14 May 2010.

42-43 Document 1– Scott, Duncan Campbell. Presentation to a House of Commons Committee. 1920. Quoted in *Belonging: The Meaning and Future of Canadian Citizenship.* Ed. William Kaplan. Montreal: McGill-Queen's, 1993. Print. Document 2 – L., Thomas. Letter to Charles Cooke. 16 Nov. 1925. Quoted in Brownlie, Robin. "'A better citizen than lots of white men': First Nations Enfranchisement—an Ontario Case Study, 1918-1940." *Canadian Historical Review* 87.1 (2006) 29-52. Print.

44-45 Document 2 – "Back in Time: Canada (1922)." *World Book Student.* Chicago, 2010. Web. 14 May 2010. Document 4 – Marlyn, John. *Under the Ribs of Death.* 1957. Toronto: McClelland and Stewart, 2010. Print.

46-47 Document 2 – Deacon, William Arthur. *Pens and Pirates.* Toronto: Ryerson, 1923. Quoted in *Interpreting Canada's Past. Volume 2, Post-Confederation.* Ed. J. M. Bumstead. 2nd ed. Toronto: Oxford, 1993. Print. Document 3 – "Exhibition of Contemporary Canadian Art Has Resulted in Fine Picture Collection." *Ottawa Citizen* 12 Jan. 1927: 4. *Google News.* Web. 28 Apr. 2010.

48-49 Document 1 – Banting, Frederick G. Nobel Lecture. 15 Sept. 1925. *Nobelprize.org.* Web. 14 May 2010.

50-51 Document 2 – Balfour Declaration of 1926. *Documenting Democracy.* Web. 14 May 2010. Document 3 – "Back in Time: United Kingdom (1926)." *World Book Student.* Chicago, 2010. Web. 14 May 2010.

52-53 Document 1 – Moore, S. J. 1929. Quoted in Thompson, John H., and Allen Seager. *Canada, 1922–1939: Decades of Discord.* Toronto: McClelland and Stewart, 1985. Print. Document 3 – Woodsworth, J. S. Speech in the House of Commons. 1931. Quoted in McNaught, Kenneth W. *A Prophet in Politics; a Biography of J. S. Woodsworth.* 1959. University of Toronto, 2001. Print.

54-55 Document 1 – King, Mackenzie. "Five-Cent Speech" in the House of Commons. 3 Apr. 1930. Quoted in Berton, Pierre. *The Great Depression, 1929-1939.* Toronto: Anchor Canada, 2001. Print. Document 3 – King, Dorothy. 1938. Quoted in *Explorations in Canadian Economic History.* Ed. Duncan Cameron. University of Ottawa, 1985. Print.

56-57 Document 1 – Statute of Westminster, 1931. In Osmanczyk, Edmund J. *Encyclopedia of the United Nations and International Agreements.* 3rd ed. Vol. 4. New York: Routledge, 2003. Print. Document 2 – "Back in Time: United Kingdom (1931)." *World Book Student.* Chicago, 2010. Web. 14 May 2010.

Additional Resources

Books

Canada Votes: How We Elect Our Government, by Linda Granfield, Kids Can Press, 2007

Desperate Glory: The Story Of WWI, by John B. Wilson, Napoleon & Company, 2008

Frederick Banting: Hero, Healer, Artist, by Stephen Eaton Hume, XYZ Publishing, 2001

The Group of Seven and Tom Thomson, by David P. Silcox, Firefly Books, 2006

The Kids' Book of Canadian History, by Carlotta Hacker, Kids Can Press, 2002

W. L. Mackenzie King, by J. L. Granatstein, Fitzhenry and Whiteside, 2002

Websites

http://www.collectionscanada.gc.ca/confederation/index-e.html
This website created by Library and Archives Canada tells the story of how Canada became a nation and describes the history of each province and territory.

http://www.collectionscanada.gc.ca/firstworldwar/index-e.html
This website about Canadians in the military includes virtual exhibitions on Canada in World War I and audio files of interviews with World War I veterans.

http://www.biographi.ca/index-e.html
The *Dictionary of Canadian Biography Online* contains biographies of important figures in Canadian history.

http://www.thecanadianencyclopedia.com/index.cfm?PgNm=TCESubjects&Params=A1
The Canadian Encyclopedia website, created by The Historica-Dominion Institute, includes articles on many Canadian topics. Users may search in English or French.

http://www.museevirtuel-virtualmuseum.ca/index-eng.jsp
This interactive website includes virtual exhibits on the Malagash Salt Mine and the Russian immigrants known as Doukhobors.

Index

Index

Acknowledgments

AKG-Images: 7 (British Library), 16 (Yvan Travert), 20 (Archives Peter Rühe), 34 (Archives Peter Rühe), 53 (Ullstein bild), 56 (Ullstein Bild); **AP Photo:** 57. **Bridgeman Art Library:** 8 (National Army Museum, London), 17 (Illustrated London News Picture Library, London), 18 (Illustrated London News Picture Library, London), 31 (Stapleton Collection); **Corbis:** 1 (Bettmann), 24 (Hulton-Deutsch Collection), 25 (Bettmann), 26 (Bettmann), 51 (Bettmann), 58 (Bettmann); **Dinodia©Link:** 4, 10, 19, 32, 54; **Getty:** 11, 13, 14, 22, 23 (Time Life Pictures), 35 (Popperfoto), 37, 38, 39, 47 (Time Life Pictures), 49, 50, 55 (Margaret Bourke-White/Time Life Pictures); **Kobal Collection:** 57; **Mary Evans Picture Library:** 42: **NGS Image Collection:** 44 (The Art Archive/Volkmar K. Wentzel), **Stewart Ross:** 15; **Topfoto:** 5 , 12, 29, 30, 33, 41, 48; **World Book:** 59.

Cover main image: **Corbis;** inset image: **League of Nations Archives, UNOG Library**